The Railway Experience

PAUL ATTERBURY

Published in Great Britain in 2017 by Shire Publications Ltd (part of Bloomsbury Publishing Plc), PO Box 883, Oxford, OX1 9PL, UK.

1385 Broadway, 5th Floor New York, NY 10018, USA.

E-mail: shire@shirebooks.co.uk
www.shirebooks.co.uk

SHIRE is a trademark of Osprey Publishing, a division of Bloomsbury Publishing Plc.

A CIP catalogue record for this book is available from the British Library.

Shire General no. 15.

ISBN-13: 978 1 78442 123 6
PDF e-book ISBN: 978 1 78442 190 8
ePub ISBN: 978 1 78442 189 2

Paul Atterbury has asserted his right under the Copyright, Designs and Patents Act, 1988, to be identified as the author of this book.

Typeset in Adobe Garamond and Kabel.
Printed in China through World Print Ltd.

Front cover: Top, see page 32–3; Bottom: Locomotive 8F 48723 at Edge Hill engine shed, February 1968. (David Christie)
Title page: On a summer's evening in about 1965, a mixed freight bound for Dundee slowly crosses the river Tay as it leaves Perth. The Class B1 locomotive is one of over 400 built between 1942 and 1952, from a Gresley design for the LNER.

17 18 19 20 21   10 9 8 7 6 5 4 3 2 1

CONTENTS

INTRODUCTION

In 1925 there were nationwide celebrations to mark the centenary of the opening of the Stockton & Darlington Railway. The focus then was on the great achievements of the Victorian and Edwardian eras. The bicentenary in 2025 should offer an opportunity to consider the achievements of this second century and to look at the ways the railways have affected the social, economic, political and technical history of modern Britain.

Luckily, a huge number of professional and amateur photographers have also been railway enthusiasts, and so the second century is well documented. Some photographs are brilliant images by famous or well-respected names, but the majority are either anonymous or bear the names of long-forgotten amateurs who nonetheless often produced fine images. It is also fortunate that, while many took the traditional three-quarter views of passing locomotives, others were keen to record the diversity of the railway scene as a whole, including buildings and structures, day-to-day operations and, above all, people at work and play.

The photographs in this book, chosen for their quality and detail, are, with a few exceptions, in the latter category. They range in date from the late Victorian era to the early 1990s, but most record the period from the 1920s to the 1970s, decades that not only witnessed great changes in the railway world but that are also within the memory span of many people alive today. Photographs are grouped in sections, covering stations and structures, railway staff at work, train and landscape views, train and infrastructure maintenance, goods and freight, high days and holidays, and the end of the line.

Left: The last steam locomotive built by British Railways was Standard Class 9F, 92220, *Evening Star*. Here in the mid-1960s, approaching the end of its active life, and looking a bit scruffy, the locomotive has paused with its passenger train at Templecombe, and a young boy makes the most of the encounter.

STATIONS AND STRUCTURES

The Euston Arch, 1950s

When completed in 1837, the Euston Arch expressed the grandiose ambitions, the pride and the achievements of the railway in early Victorian Britain. Designed by Philip Hardwick, it celebrated the arrival in London of the London & Birmingham Railway whose terminus station, the first in the capital, had opened the previous year. It was a Doric portico, a great classical triumphal arch of which the ancient Greeks would have been proud. It immediately became a major London landmark, and was much loved as a powerful symbol of Victorian greatness for over a century, despite increasing amounts of grime and the construction of encroaching buildings.

The decision in 1961 to pull it down, along with the grand station behind it, was announced by a British Railways Board increasingly driven by a modernisation plan that was determined to remove the old-fashioned image associated with the network's Victorian heritage. The outcry that followed the announcement took BR by surprise, and it was the start of a battle, with the arch becoming an instantly recognisable symbol in the struggle against perceived corporate vandalism and greed. It was a long, hard-fought and ultimately unsuccessful campaign, with the final decision made by Prime Minister Harold Macmillan. With the arch went the iron trainshed of 1837 and the magnificent Great Hall of 1849, all to be replaced by a bland and uncomfortable modern station clearly inspired by an airport terminal.

This 1950s photograph shows the arch as it was known to most Londoners, a vast and gloomy, though enduringly popular, lump of decorative architecture. With its flanking pavilions, the Euston Arch was a classic London postcard image, and thus familiar to travellers all over the world.

Victoria Station, London, July 1927

Victoria Station is London's most memorable monument to railway rivalry. It is actually two stations built side by side by rival companies and until 1924 there was no connection between them. Anyone wanting to pass from one to the other had to go out into the street and use the main entrance. For decades this confused foreigners and others not used to the eccentric layout.

First on the site was the London, Brighton and South Coast Railway (L. B, & S.C.R.), whose iron trainshed, functional but impressive, was completed on the western side in 1860, followed a year later by the grand French-style Grosvenor Hotel, which was run independently until 1899. Next, in 1862, came the London, Chatham and Dover Railway, with a much more elegant trainshed, in arched iron and glass, designed by their engineer Sir John Fowler. Separating the two stations was a solid wall. Their equally separate façades were by contrast rather inadequate, and increasingly tatty wooden structures. First to address this was the L. B & S.C.R., whose massive new nine-storey brick and stone frontage, a striking design by Sir Charles Morgan in Edwardian Baroque, was completed in 1907. A year later, the Dover company, by then renamed the South Eastern and Chatham Railway, completed their new façade, a magnificent French-style stone building designed by A.W. Blomfield. In 1923 the two rivals became part of the Southern Railway, and in due course British Railways, but, apart from opening up walkways through the dividing wall, little was done to alter the two stations until 1979 when the Brighton line's trainshed was removed and replaced by a shop and office complex above the platforms.

This 1927 photograph shows the now lost Brighton trainshed. With sunlight shining through the glass roof, this photograph must have been taken early one morning. There is practically no-one to be seen, but a long line of taxis wait while the Southern Railway's smart locomotives simmer.

Bristol Temple Meads Station, February 1973

For the Victorians, the railway station was a new building type and so, with no models to follow, engineers and architects rose to the challenge with imagination. During the early decades of the railway age Classical and Gothic styles tended to be favoured, though Italianate, French and Renaissance were not unknown. Isambard Kingdom Brunel was keen on Tudor, the British version of Gothic, and so the station he designed for the Bristol terminus of his Great Western Railway was in this style, complete with a hammer beam roof. It was completed in 1840 and three years later an adjacent terminus, set at a right angle, was opened for the Bristol and Exeter Railway. Even when ultimately connected by a sharp curve, operations were complex and so in the early 1870s the GWR decided to rebuild the station. The architect was Matthew Digby Wyatt, and his spectacular French Gothic building was opened in 1878.

Formed from grey and white stone with chequerboard effects, the station, rising high above the long approach slope, featured a central tower, capped with a French-style pavilion, flanking side spires and a wealth of battlements, mullion windows, crockets and other decorative details. Outside, ridge-and-furrow-glazed iron canopies gave shelter to passengers. In 1935 the station was expanded, with more platforms added. The tower's pavilion was removed and some of the carving simplified, but little else was changed and so Temple Meads remains one of Britain's best Gothic stations, famous for its decoration, its lofty ticket hall and the great curving span of the iron and glass trainshed.

On a cold, clear day in February 1973, the midday sun is showing Temple Meads' recently cleaned façade at its best, highlighting all the Gothic detail. Three taxis seem sufficient for the few passengers, though the short-term car park is busy.

Peterborough North Station, 25 May 1963

The Eastern Counties Railway opened Peterborough's first station in June 1845, on its line from Ely. Other railways used it, including the London and Birmingham's Northampton to Peterborough route. The Great Northern Railway, building its line southwards towards London, built its own station, which opened in August 1850. This had various names, including Peterborough Cowgate and Peterborough Priestgate, but when the London & Northeast Railway (LNER) took over both stations in 1923 it decided to call them Peterborough East and Peterborough North. Things remained much the same until the 1960s, when Peterborough East Station was closed, along with some of the lines served by Peterborough North.

The disadvantages of Peterborough North became increasingly apparent. It was on a cramped site with few platforms, and thus a likely bottleneck on the planned upgrading of the East Coast main line. A programme of total rebuilding began in the 1970s, which continued in stages until 2013.

The result is that practically nothing from this 1963 view survives. The trainshed over the platforms was demolished, and the new station is now well to the left. The photograph is full of period detail. A London-bound express is passing through the station, headed by an LNER-designed Class A1 Pacific locomotive, No. 60141, *Abbotsford*. Meanwhile, barrows piled with mail sacks are being loaded onto carriages in the bay platform, and a diesel shunter waits to bring old carriages out of a siding. A platform water tower and telegraph poles densely laden with insulators are further reminders of a long-lost railway age.

Marlborough Station, 23 May 1929

The daily lives of small country towns throughout Britain were changed beyond recognition by the coming of the railway. Typical is Marlborough in Wiltshire, where the first station was opened in 1864, the end of a branch line from Savernake financed largely by local businessmen. It was operated by the Great Western Railway (GWR), who took control in 1886. Meanwhile, a second station had been opened in the town, on a line built by the ambitious but underfunded Swindon, Marlborough and Andover company, which in due course became part of the Midland and South Western Junction Railway. Thus, from the 1880s Marlborough was served by two stations, a not uncommon situation in late Victorian Britain. In the 1920s both came under the control of the GWR, who named them Marlborough High Level and Marlborough Low Level. In 1933 the GWR closed the original, High Level, station to passengers, though goods continued for a while, and then in 1961 the Low Level station and all its connecting lines were closed, isolating Marlborough from the railway network.

This 1929 photograph shows High Level, the town's branch line terminus station, four years before its closure to passengers. The photographer will have stood on the track in front of an old GWR tank locomotive, which is waiting to work the train back to Savernake. Everything is clean and tidy and the stationmaster, the signalman – standing outside his platform box – the driver and the fireman all pose for the camera. Only the porter hides his face as he leans against the fluted iron column of the magnificent platform lamp. Though suffering increasingly from road competition, the railway was still at the social and economic heart of its community, and a sense of pride, a legacy of the Victorian era, is still apparent.

Worlington Golf Links Halt, 23 April 1960

Few small communities in late Victorian England were far from a station. This was the great age of the branch line – short, often locally funded railways which linked small towns and villages to the national network. Some were built as branches, while others were part of grander schemes that were never completed. Typical of the latter was the Mildenhall branch, planned originally by the Great Eastern Railway as part of a secondary route between Cambridge and Norwich. When the line reached Mildenhall in 1885, the plan was abandoned and so it became a rural branch serving the agricultural needs of a remote part of England.

In its length of just under 21 miles, the Mildenhall branch included three intermediate stations, Fen Ditton Halt, Exning Road Halt and Worlington Golf Links Halt, all designed to serve isolated communities along the route. These were very basic stations, without proper platforms or shelters and marked only by a name board and a lamp. Trains included a carriage with extra steps, to enable passengers to join or leave the train at these minimal halts.

On an April day in 1960 a surprising number of passengers are waiting for one of the three daily trains at Worlington Golf Links Halt. Some have children and another is elderly and so the guard is ready to give them a hand. None look like golfers, though the nearby Royal Worlington & Newmarket Golf Club, founded in 1893, and the home club for the Cambridge University Golf Team, was the station's main *raison d'être*. Just over two years after the photograph was taken the whole Mildenhall branch line was closed to passengers.

The Tay Bridge, c. 1898

On 28 December 1879, the 5.27pm train from Burntisland to Dundee, carrying about seventy-six people, set off across the Tay Bridge. A wild gale was blowing along the river, and thus directly at the bridge. After a few minutes the train was seen to vanish into the water, along with the high girders section of the bridge. At the enquiry, structural failure was blamed, and Sir Thomas Bouch, the engineer who had designed the bridge, was disgraced and ruined. He died within the year.

Opened for passenger services in June 1878, the single-track bridge, which was over two miles long, had been considered one of the wonders of the railway world. After the disaster, the North British Railway determined to replace the bridge. This new twin-track bridge was completed in 1887, and has successfully carried large numbers of trains ever since.

Clearly visible are the seventy-four spans, supported on twin wrought-iron cylinders, stretching out across the river towards Dundee. The high girder section, to allow the passage of ships, can be seen in the distance. The remains of the supporting piers for the old bridge are on the right. The main line continues due south from the bridge towards Edinburgh, while Wormit Station, in the foreground, is the start of a branch line eastwards along the coast to Tayport, closed in 1969.

The photograph, dating from about 1898, is full of interesting details, including advertisements for Venus Soap, DCL Malt Extract, Melrose Teas and Pattison Scotch Whisky, a short-lived brand only available from 1896 to 1898. There is a tidy flowerbed at the end of the station building, and a wheelbarrow and tools are neatly stacked, but there is no sign of life.

Signal Gantry at Southampton Central, 30 August 1965

The movement of trains has long been controlled by manually operated semaphore signals and, although electronic coloured light signalling was developed quite early on, the traditional signal remained in use through the twentieth century and is still in operation in remote parts of the network. In the 1960s massive signal gantries like this could still be seen on main lines and at busy stations all over Britain, controlled from the large signal boxes that were then an essential part of any station complex. The linkage rods that operate the signals and points are visible in the foreground, each connected to a large lever in the signal box. Though reflective of modern technology, these signals were surprisingly traditional in appearance, with each one sporting a decorative finial.

On a summer's day in 1965 the 1.30pm Waterloo to Weymouth express, probably filled with holidaymakers on their way to Dorset and Channel Island resorts, has paused at Southampton Central while West Country Class No. 34046, *Braunton*, takes on water. This familiar scene was soon to disappear, with steam haulage ending on the Southern Region of British Railways in 1967. This procedure has attracted the attention of a few passengers along the platform, while an enthusiast, suitably dressed in a long raincoat despite the sunny day, has gone down the platform slope for a better view.

Today this service is operated by modern Class 444 trains, the line having been electrified to Bournemouth in 1967 and Weymouth in 1988. Southampton Central Station looks much the same, though the signal gantry is long gone, along with everything to do with the steam age.

NOTICE
IT IS STRICTLY
PROHIBITED TO
RIDE MOTORCYCLES
SCOOTERS, BICYCLES
OR SIMILAR
VEHICLES THROUGH
WICKET GATES

3818

Tramway Junction Level Crossing, Gloucester, 21 September 1964

Britain still has over 6,000 level crossings and when this photograph was taken, there were many thousands more. Tramway, or Horton Road, level crossing, at the eastern end of Gloucester Station, was always a notorious bottleneck as most trains entering or leaving Gloucester Station had to pass through it. The name comes from the Gloucester and Cheltenham Tramway, a horse-drawn coal and stone line in operation from 1811 to 1861, whose route crossed the main railway near the level crossing.

On a sunny September day an assorted group of pedestrians and cyclists wait at the crossing, something they would all have been used to doing as the gates were so often closed. Idly, they watch the passing train, which is headed by a scruffy Class 2800 locomotive, No. 3818. This elderly workhorse was from a large group of similar 2-8-0 locomotives whose origins go back to a Churchward design of 1903. Signal box and signals, a gas lamp probably converted to electricity, the old wooden crossing gate, a hand-painted sign and a background of gasometers rising above a muddle of old brick buildings all add a sense of period to a view that is now completely changed. In the 1960s so many railway scenes still echoed Victorian Britain, and had a particular enduring quality. Today, practically everything in the photograph has gone. There is still a level crossing on Horton Road but there are fewer trains and the modern barriers sit in a much more empty landscape. Cars, notably absent in the 1964 photograph, now dominate the scene.

Cayton Signal Box, Yorkshire, 1970s

Today, the signal box, one of the most characteristic features of the railway landscape, is almost extinct on the national network. In 1948 there were over 10,000 in use throughout Britain, but by 2012 this had been reduced to 500. Since then, the number has continued to fall rapidly as large centralised electronic control centres have come into operation. Today, traditional signal boxes are to be found mostly on a few rural lines and heritage railways. Some classic examples on the national network have been given listed status by Historic England, and equivalent organisations in Wales and Scotland.

Most boxes were constructed by private companies but conformed to a general pattern: a two-storey structure with the brick- or stone-built lower part housing the interlocking machinery and a glazed timber upper part for the signalman and his equipment. Many designs were used, with attractive variations in the decorative detail, notably window styles, barge boarding and roof finials. Later, more standard designs began to emerge, particularly from the 1920s.

This 1970s photograph shows the small timber-clad box at Cayton, near Scarborough in Yorkshire, with the signalman watching from the window. Traditional details include the roof finials and the crossing gate, complete with lamp. In the background is the station house, now a private residence, dating from the opening of Cayton station by the York & North Midland Railway in 1846. Today, the box has gone and the line, though still in use, has been single-tracked. The station closed in 1952.

Irwell Bridge Signal Box, Manchester, 1920s

In the early days of the railway, train control systems were erratic and inconsistent and there were frequent accidents. By the 1850s the block system of train operation was being used, with sections of track controlled by signal boxes linked by telegraph, and with interlocked points and signals. Soon this became the standard for the whole network. Signal boxes had glazed upper sections, to give the signalman good all-round visibility and to allow communication with passing train crews. The internal space was well organised to enable easy access to all the operating levers for the signals and points, telegraph machines, bells, telephones and everything else involved in train control. There was also a raised and well-lit desk for ledgers and paperwork. Creature comforts usually included a stove and basic catering facilities for the signalmen, who could spend long, lonely periods of duty in remote locations.

The signalman's responsibilities were considerable and included the management of all trains passing through the section controlled by the box, the detailed recording of all traffic and all signal messages sent and received, the communications by telegraph with other boxes and stations, the basic maintenance of the signals and other equipment, and the care of the lamps used on the signals, the operation of level crossings and looking after incidents such as train breakdowns.

A large and busy box like Irwell Bridge could have around a hundred levers, some of which are seen in use in this 1920s photograph, with the telegraph machines ranged on shelves above them. As expected, the interior is tidy and spotlessly clean.

RAILWAY STAFF

London & South Western Railway Locomotive, c. 1900

An immaculate Class 445 express passenger locomotive waits at an unknown location. One of twelve similar locomotives, designed by William Adams for the London & South Western Railway, and built by Robert Stephenson and Company, No. 448 was new in about 1883. It remained in use until the mid 1920s, having passed with the rest of the class to the Southern Railway in 1923.

Carefully posed and well-detailed portrait photographs of railway locomotives were a popular phenomenon through the late nineteenth and early twentieth centuries, often taken for the records when new. In this case, No. 448 was clearly not new, and so its fine condition reflected the hard work put in by the staff of the shed where it was based, and the pride that was an integral part of railway employment at that time.

The photograph is actually as much about the driver and the fireman. At that time, a main line express driver was a man of great experience and responsibility, highly respected and with a well-defined position, not only in the railway hierarchy but also in society. The fireman, though usually a trainee driver, and equally skilled in the operation of the locomotive, was in every way a lesser being. Driver and fireman stand far apart, their respective positions defined by their pose and their different uniforms. Their relationship was formal, professional, respectful and mutually dependent, but probably without friendship. Yet the successful operation of their locomotive in changing and challenging circumstances was based on their being able to work together over long hours on the confined, uncomfortable and often dangerous footplate.

The Flying Scotsman, 1 May 1928

In 1862 the first Special Scotch Express ran between London and Edinburgh, a journey that took over ten hours. By the 1870s this service was known unofficially as the 'Flying Scotsman' but the name was not formally adopted until 1924. The same year a recently built Class A1 locomotive was given the same name, and the LNER number 4472, to publicise the Flying Scotsman service.

At 10am on 1 May 1928, the *Flying Scotsman* left London King's Cross at the start of the first non-stop London to Edinburgh service. Scheduled to take eight hours, this was at the time the longest non-stop passenger service in the world. It was made possible by a special tender, enlarged to carry more coal, built with a narrow corridor along one side and connected to the passenger coaches, allowing the locomotive's crew to be changed en route. A number of similar tenders were built to allow the LNER, and later British Railways, to operate various non-stop services linking London and Edinburgh. On this inaugural run, the Flying Scotsman service was hauled by the *Flying Scotsman* locomotive.

This LNER publicity photograph shows the *Flying Scotsman* ready to depart from King's Cross. A crowd of onlookers has gathered on the platform, including lucky schoolboy enthusiasts in caps and a lady in a smart hat. The *Flying Scotsman*'s driver, Albert Pibworth, wearing his old overall jacket over a clean white shirt and tie, smiles at the camera, while bowler-hatted Sir Nigel Gresley, the locomotive's designer and the LNER's Chief Mechanical Engineer, stands behind him. To the left, and peering through the cab window of a crowded footplate, is the Lord Mayor of London, Sir Kynaston Studd.

Fred and Jim at Crewe, 1950s

A steam engine is a relatively simple machine and, if well maintained, it can operate efficiently over long periods of time. Driving a steam locomotive, at first sight a straightforward operation, is actually a complex activity in which knowledge of the route and its signals and stations, and good time-keeping were the easy bits. Much more challenging were the external factors that could affect the locomotive's performance, including maintenance, type of coal, weather, quality of water, gradients, the weight of the train, the fitness of the footplate crew and the state of the track, and so good driving was all about anticipation.

A trainee driver started as a cleaner in a locomotive shed, a filthy and demanding job which included clearing out the firebox, cleaning, oiling and polishing the locomotive, inside and out, checking coal and water, and laying and lighting the fire. All this gave a trainee a complete knowledge of a locomotive's inner workings and habits. The next step was to become a fireman, initially on locomotives around the shed and the sidings, and then gradually onto the main line. Over several years, through observation, guidance and experience, a fireman could become a driver.

A good working relationship on the footplate was essential, based on respect and a mutual dependency, with a driver willing to teach and a fireman willing to learn. Drivers knew how to be firemen, but firemen had to learn to drive. A good footplate crew could by this time combine professionalism with friendship. This photograph, taken at Crewe in the 1950s, shows driver Fred Handley, and his trainee fireman Jim Carter, then aged seventeen and at the start of his career.

Locomotive on the Turntable at York, 5 October 1936

From the start steam locomotives had to be regularly turned round, and so the turntable was born. At first these were simple rotating platforms, set into stretches of track at stations, locomotive sheds and goods yards. As locomotives became steadily heavier and larger, so the need grew for bigger and better engineered turntables, able to rotate on rails around a central pivot point, and serving two or more sets of track. The first turntables were about 20–30 feet across but by the 1920s and 1930s, the diameter had reached over 60 feet.

Turntables were installed at termini and other major stations, at junctions and goods yards, and at many engine sheds. Early examples were hand-operated but, as the scale increased and the engineering became more complex, some form of mechanical power was required. Geared windlass operation was in time replaced by motor drives powered either by vacuum pressure from the locomotive or electricity. The need for turntables diminished as diesel and electric locomotives took over, and the once-universal turntables are now only to be found on heritage lines.

Turning their locomotive was one of the many tasks undertaken by the footplate crew. When this photograph was taken, most major turntables were mechanically powered, though some large hand-operated examples were still in use. In 1936 York still had one and using it must have been an unwelcome addition to a long shift. Here the driver and fireman are working hard to turn their locomotive, a nearly new Class 5, No. 5093, which weighed about 72 tons. The Black Fives, as they were known, were a very successful locomotive type designed by William Stanier for the LMS, with 842 built between 1934 and 1951.

Diesel Locomotive Driver, c. 1960

The first diesel-powered railway vehicles were built before the First World War but until the 1930s the use of diesel power was limited. The first main line diesel electric locomotives were developed in Russia and the United States, and other countries soon followed. In Britain progress was slow, though the LMS operated diesel locomotives in the late 1930s. The real boost came with British Railways' 1955 modernisation plan, with its planned transition from steam to diesel and electric power. The development of a wide range of diesel locomotive classes and types followed, including diesel mechanical, diesel electric and diesel hydraulic.

Through this period many steam drivers were retrained to drive diesel and electric locomotives, and the transition must have been a pleasant experience. A warm, comfortable and clean cab replaced the challenging environment of the footplate, a fuel tank filled at the depot replaced water and coal, and instead of the challenge of the steam engine there was a modern, responsive and permanently powerful locomotive that could be driven from either end.

Many of the new locomotives were used throughout the British Railways network, but even in the era of nationalisation the Western Region, the former GWR, managed to retain a degree of individuality. From the late 1950s several diesel hydraulic locomotive types were developed by the Region for its own use, and these helped retain its traditional sense of independence.

This BR publicity photograph shows a former steam driver at the controls of one of these Western Region locomotives, with the past represented by a classic GWR steam locomotive in the background.

Token Exchange at Pentir Rhiw, 24 August 1961

The control of trains operating on single-track lines always posed problems and at first pilotmen accompanied every train. Later, wood or metal staffs were used, identified to each section of track, and only the train carrying the staff could proceed along that section. Once block signalling and electric interlocking had been developed, train movements were controlled by tablets or tokens issued from interlocked instruments that ensured that only one could be in use at any one time on a particular section of the route.

The main problem, not really addressed until the twentieth century, was that the tablet, staff or token had to be exchanged by hand, either between passing trains at a station, or between the train crew and a signalman. This was a process fraught with difficulties and dangers, particularly in bad weather or at night. Automatic exchange systems were developed but these were often too expensive for minor and rural routes. The real change came with the introduction of the radio-controlled electronic block system, with drivers being given permission to proceed by displays in the cab controlled by a central computer.

On a murky summer's day in 1961 at Pentir Rhiw Station, on the rural route between Brecon and Merthyr, the train driver or fireman and the signalman prepare to exchange tokens, to enable the train to enter the next single-line section. The tokens are attached to a large loop, to facilitate the exchange. In some places, there were hooks to catch the loop and sometimes the signalman would lean out of his window to catch it on his arm. This extraordinarily old-fashioned practice is now largely confined to heritage lines.

Wagon Checking, Monmouth, February 1951

The railways have always been major employers. In 1855 the total number employed was 98,000 and by 1884 this had risen to 368,000. When the nationalised British Railways took control of the network in 1948, it had 650,000 men and women on its books. By 1994, when the railways were privatised, this had fallen to 116,000.

Within those numbers were a diverse variety of jobs, many of which were invisible to the ordinary rail user. This applied particularly to the freight sector, until the 1950s the railways' major creator of income. Many railways were built primarily for the transport of freight, and the management of this traffic was complex and expensive in employment terms. In the pre-computer age every wagon and every item of freight had to be manually tracked and recorded as it passed through the system. Something loaded in Penzance and destined for Inverness had to be fully documented at every stage of its journey, a process that inevitably involved changes of wagon or train.

In addition, all wagons had to have maintenance schedules that were regularly brought up to date. Failed wagons caused expensive delays and disruption, and so frequent visual checks were also carried out while wagons were standing in sidings, or waiting in loading bays or marshalling yards. This photograph shows Harry George, a wheel-tapper and wagon checker, at work in the wagon sidings at Monmouth Troy Station in February 1951. With his long tapping hammer under his arm, he is noting faults on an old LMS-built plank wagon owned by Bairds & Dalmellington Limited, an Ayrshire iron, coal and brick company.

Signal Maintenance, 1950s

When railways started there were no signals; much of the control of trains was carried out by stationmasters and policemen. As signals and signal boxes began to be used, so the policemen moved into the boxes and became signalmen. From the 1850s signalling and train control systems became more standardised, and so a number of specialist manufacturers were set up to produce signalling equipment for the railway companies, both mechanical and electrical.

At the end of the nineteenth century the first power-driven signalling equipment came onto the market, using hydraulics and electricity, but mechanical systems remained in use through the twentieth century, particularly on country and branch lines. The rules and regulations associated with the correct operation of a signal box were extensive and complex, and signalmen were expected to attend training schools, with regular refresher courses and examinations, along with various grades of responsibility.

Maintenance was always important, and most railway companies had signal and telegraph departments that looked after their own network. However, day-to-day maintenance was part of the long list of duties for which signalmen were responsible. This included looking after the signal lamps, cleaning, oiling and greasing the many mechanical linkages between the levers and the signals and points, and carrying out straightforward running repairs. These tasks involved regular use of the steep signal ladders, often in the dark or in bad weather.

This 1950s photograph shows a signalman tightening bolts on a signal, probably a constant problem with mechanical components and connections.

Loading Parcels into a Passenger Train, Derby, 24 May 1934

Through the nineteenth century there were constant battles between the Post Office and the railways concerning the carriage of parcels, only partly resolved by legislation such as the Post Office (Parcels) Act of 1892. The railways had always carried parcels and, until the 1870s, the Post Office's remit was largely limited to letters. When the Post Office did start a parcel service, it could not handle large, bulky, heavy or difficult items, and so these remained with the railways.

For reasons of speed and efficiency, railways carried much of their parcel traffic in the guards' compartment in passenger trains, and one of the many responsibilities of the guard was looking after these parcels. This included loading them or managing their loading correctly and safely, and making sure that they were unloaded at the right station. On a busy line, these activities could take up much of the guard's time, and so delays at stations while parcels were loaded and unloaded were not uncommon. For this, and other reasons, the railways introduced dedicated parcels trains on many routes.

The sheer diversity of what could be called a parcel was remarkable. The guard could have in his compartment, along with conventional parcels, eggs and other comestibles, machine parts, clothing, documents, coal and other goods in sacks, builders' materials, bicycles and sporting goods, unaccompanied passengers' luggage and even small livestock, such as chickens, ducks, pigeons or rabbits.

Here, in 1934, a member of the LMS platform staff at Derby is busy checking and loading a typically diverse range of parcels into the guard's compartment, a job undertaken by porters at large stations.

LOCOMOTIVE VIEWS
Eastbound Express, Cole, Somerset, 22 September 1962

In a classic steam age photograph, a London-bound express races along the GWR main line from Taunton, with clouds of smoke and steam showing that the locomotive and its crew were working hard. The smartly presented locomotive, No. 5992, *Holton Hall*, was one of the 259 members of the 4900, or Hall Class built between 1924 and 1943. Designed by Charles Collett for the Great Western Railway, this was a remarkably successful and popular locomotive class throughout the GWR and British Railways eras. *Holton Hall* was built at Swindon in 1939 and withdrawn in 1965.

Cole, near Bruton, was always a popular spot with enthusiasts and trainspotters because of the nearby bridge carrying the Somerset & Dorset's Bath to Bournemouth line across the GWR's tracks. Cole Station, just south of the bridge, was between Evercreech Junction and Templecombe, both exciting places for Somerset & Dorset enthusiasts. In the autumn of 1962 steam was still dominant on both routes. The boys watching would have been able to see and enjoy not only the many Halls, Manors and other great GWR locomotives passing to and fro between the West Country and Paddington, but also the more varied locomotives crossing the bridge while working the challenging and hilly S&D route, where freight and passenger trains were often double-headed.

The Somerset & Dorset closed in 1966, and much of the route has disappeared. Cole's station building survives, as a private house, and the traces of the bridge that carried the S&D over the GWR line can still be spotted by the sharp-eyed enthusiast from the windows of modern fast-moving diesels.

Afternoon School Train in Glen Ogle, May 1960

Perhaps the greatest legacy of the Victorian railway builders was not the famous main lines, but the amazing network of country and rural railways and branch lines that covered the map of Britain. These were the social and economic heart of the nation. By 1910, when the system was at its peak, few places were very far from some kind of railway connection. By 1962 much of this network was still in place. Hundreds of miles had been lost through various closures but this was the calm before the storm, when the values of the Victorian railway system were still largely unchallenged. A year later, the publication of the Beeching Report was to launch a closure programme destined to decimate the railways of Britain.

On a sunny spring day in 1960 all this seems very far away, as the 4.05pm school train from Callander to Killin climbs slowly through Glen Ogle. At the head of the single carriage is a small 0-4-4 tank locomotive, No. 55263, a member of a class originally designed by the Caledonian Railway in 1900 for rural and branch line use. In 1925 a slightly revised version was developed and this locomotive is from that batch. Built in Manchester, it enjoyed a long life, based mostly at Oban.

However, this idyllic version of the country railway at its best was not to last. Just over a year later, in November 1961, No. 55263 was withdrawn and cut up. The completion of the Callander & Oban Railway in 1880 had made possible the construction of a branch line to Killin and Loch Tay and this was opened in 1886. For years it served Killin and the town thrived, with an expanding tourist trade visiting Loch Tay. By the 1950s a steady decline had set in and the Callander & Oban line, along with the Killin branch, closed in September 1965.

Silver Jubilee, 1935

In the 1920s and 1930s many photographers and some painters, particularly in the United States, were fascinated by the machinery of steam as a reflection of the modern industrial age. This image, with its emphasis on the locomotive's driving wheels and connecting rods, is typical of that fascination.

The locomotive is *Silver Jubilee*, from a new class of main line passenger locomotives designed for the LMS by William Stanier and built from 1934. At first, they were a development of the Patriot class but from 1935 they were established as a class of their own, when No. 45552, the first of the class, was given the Silver Jubilee name, to mark the Silver Jubilee that year of King George V and Queen Mary. From that moment, the class became known as Jubilees, and by 1938 the LMS had built 191 of them, all of which were transferred to British Railways in 1948. Originally, they were painted in LMS crimson lake.

At first, names given to the locomotives were drawn from countries and places in the British Empire, reflecting the Jubilee celebrations. Later, they commemorated famous admirals, naval battles and warships, early locomotives and Northern Irish provinces.

This photograph may show *Silver Jubilee* at the time of its naming in 1935. Certainly, this quality of finish was exceptional, particularly for a locomotive that had already been in service prior to being named. Strangely, *Silver Jubilee* was not selected for preservation, despite being the first of its class. Withdrawn in 1964, it was broken up a year later.

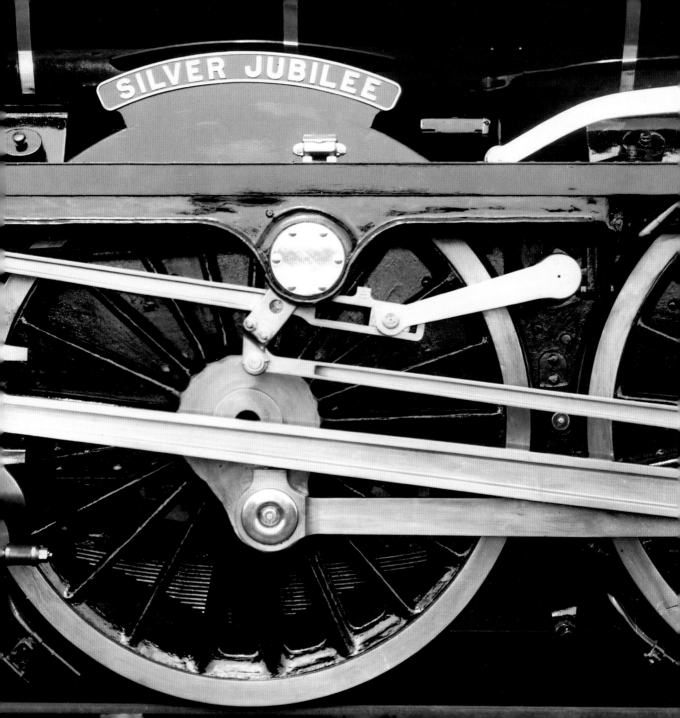

Railway and Canal near Wigan, early 1970s

On a summer's day in the early 1970s, a passenger train hauled by a Class 47 diesel locomotive, in the plain blue British Rail corporate livery introduced from 1962, approaches Wigan, with the distinctive spire of early nineteenth-century St Catherine's Church in the background. In the foreground is the Leeds and Liverpool Canal, with a small steel narrowboat making its way towards the railway bridge. Boys stand and watch by the lock, possibly Hell Meadow.

This scene, a classic conjunction of canal and railway, is one to be found all over Britain, but particularly in industrial areas. The Leeds and Liverpool, whose 127-mile trans-Pennine route is one of the most challenging in the British canal network, was not completed until 1816, by which time the railway age was only a couple of decades away. However, the canal was initially successful, thanks in part to its broad locks, and dividends were paid well into the 1820s. Increasing railway competition through the Victorian era brought about a slow decline, but commercial traffic survived on the canal into the twentieth century. By the 1970s the emphasis had shifted to leisure usage, and the Leeds and Liverpool, along with many other canals, found a new lease of life.

It is difficult to date this photograph precisely, though the graffiti gives clues. 'LFC' (Liverpool Football Club) is not very helpful but the adjacent 'Slade' is more useful, as the group was at its peak between 1971 and 1974. The anti-American Vietnam slogans on the bridge, looking quite freshly painted, obviously pre-date the final end of the war in 1975.

MAINTENANCE

Stoke-on-Trent Locomotive Shed, late 1950s or early 1960s

Steam locomotives required regular maintenance, both in use and when at rest. Supplies of coal and water were essential, along with cleaning and the oiling and greasing of the many moving parts. The driver and fireman, whose roster would start and end at the locomotive shed, would have been responsible for much of this.

Sheds – or to use their more formal title, motive power depots – were places where locomotives could be stored, maintained, serviced and repaired. There were hundreds all over Britain, ranging from single locomotive ones at the ends of branch lines to massive facilities fully equipped for heavy engineering. They came in various shapes and styles, from the early roundhouse type to long, linear structures through which locomotives could be driven. The management of the larger sheds was complex, with locomotives coming in and out of use, being moved around for water and coal and being repaired or stored. Visiting locomotives also needed to be looked after. All locomotives had a home shed, and each carried a shed plate on their smokebox door.

A large linear shed was Stoke-on-Trent, shed plate 5D, seen here in the late 1950s or early 1960s. The arrangement of densely packed locomotives, of many types for different traffic requirements, and facing in both directions, is typical for a shed of this size. It is probably early morning as all have been coaled and several are being prepared for use. There are a number of familiar LMS-designed classes, including Black Fives, a 2-8-0 8F, and a 1920s 2-6-4 Fairburn tank, along with a more modern British Railways Standard locomotive. At the back are two lines of older locomotives, stored out of use or waiting to be scrapped.

A Locomotive Roundhouse, early 1960s

The railway age generated a number of new building types, both commercial and industrial. The prime example is the station, and its related buildings, but also important were technical structures such as locomotive sheds, the most distinctive of which is the roundhouse.

The first roundhouse, in which locomotives were housed on tracks radiating out from a central turntable, was probably that built by the North Midland Railway in Derby in 1839. This structure, 190 feet in diameter, and covered with a dome-shaped roof, had sixteen radiating tracks, each capable of storing two locomotives. The idea of the roundhouse spread quickly, with many being built in Britain, Europe and in other parts of the world, notably in North America. Generally circular or semicircular in form, roundhouses steadily increased in size, with twenty or more tracks spreading outwards. Their small size and resulting operational complexity soon made many early examples obsolete and so today few survive; only one in Britain, Barrow Hill in Derbyshire, is still in railway use. Other survivors have mostly been converted to other purposes.

This dramatic photograph shows a large roundhouse, probably in the early 1960s. Shafts of sunlight hit the central turntable, as two elderly drivers walk away at the end of their shifts. Steam and diesel locomotives lurk in the shadows, while steam drifts from a recently used locomotive. In the foreground is one of the track pits used for cleaning and maintenance, surrounded by pools of oily water. A roundhouse, often a difficult working environment, could also be dangerous because of the movement of locomotives and the turntable activity.

Coal and Water, West Hartlepool, 1960s

Steam locomotives consume prodigious quantities of coal and water and so they had either to carry enough for the day's work or replenish supplies along their route. Most locomotives hauled a tender carrying tons of coal and thousands of gallons of water, and it would start the day having been fully loaded at the shed. Coal was loaded mechanically at large sheds, and by hand at smaller ones, and the tender usually carried sufficient for the journey, or day's work. Water supplies had to be regularly replenished and so many stations and freight yards were equipped with various forms of water tower. Water troughs, laid between the rails on major routes, enabled the tender to be refilled via a scoop while the train was travelling at speed. Tank locomotives had coal bunkers at the rear and water tanks, usually either side of, or across, the boiler. The many duties of the fireman while the locomotive was in use included filling the tender or the tanks with water, looking after the coal supply, shovelling tons of coal into the firebox while maintaining both the quality of the fire and the steam pressure, and running the injectors to pump water from the tender or tanks into the boiler.

Here at West Hartlepool shed, an elderly and rather decrepit Class Q6 locomotive, No. 63368, one of a class of 120 built for heavy freight use between 1913 and 1921, is being prepared for its day's work. Coal is being loaded manually via a wheeled hopper, probably by the fireman. When this task is complete, he will use the water tower to fill the tender's water tank. The driver is on the footplate, looking after the fire and the steam pressure, and perhaps brewing some tea. A successful and popular class, the Q6s lived on into the British Railways era, with some surviving in use until 1967.

Cleaning an LNER Locomotive, 1930s

Drivers and firemen started their careers as locomotive cleaners, usually as school leavers or apprentices. Organised into gangs of about six, they were given from the start the dirtiest jobs, such as cleaning the locomotive and tender wheels, inside and out. In the course of a day's work, which started very early, they would empty the firebox and clean it, along with all the inside workings of the locomotive, including the smokebox. Every inch of the outside would then be cleaned and polished, including the paintwork and the connecting rods, and the buffers. By this means, the cleaners would learn and understand the design and function of every bit of the locomotive. As they progressed, they would learn to service and maintain the locomotive, to lay and light the fire, and build up the steam pressure. After a long period of training as a cleaner, they would face examinations, both practical and on the rule book, and then, if all was well, they would begin to fire locomotives on shed or shunting duties. From here, there was a gradual progression to main line firing and, after about seven years, to driving.

Several cleaning gangs were employed in the larger sheds and there was always rivalry between them, with rewards going to those who turned out the smartest locomotive. This photograph, taken at a major London LNER shed in the 1930s, shows members of a cleaning gang at work on the paintwork and metalwork of a large express locomotive. They are working hard to make the locomotive look its best when it goes on duty. The next day they will have to do it all over again, a repetitive process that gradually built up a deep knowledge of locomotive operation, along with a pride in the railway and the way of life it represented.

Weed-killing on the Southern Railway, 1920s

Steel rails carried on wooden sleepers set into deep ballast might not seem to offer ideal growing conditions for plants, but controlling weed growth along the track has always been a problem for railway companies, particularly on lesser used lines and sidings. In fact, it has long been known that the wind generated by passing trains is a very effective way of disseminating plant seeds.

The classic case history is that of *Senecio squalidus*, better known as Oxford ragwort. Introduced to Britain from Sicily early in the eighteenth century, the plant was established early in the Botanic Gardens in Oxford. It escaped from here to spread across Oxford but, with the coming of the railway, it was able to spread much more effectively across the whole country, finding railway track ballast an adequate substitute for the volcanic ash of its Sicilian homeland.

Maintenance of the steel rails, the sleepers and the stone ballast that make up the track has always been vital to the successful operation of a railway. Initially, track maintenance was the responsibility of gangers, or linesmen, who until the late nineteenth century worked without any kind of mechanical help. Their duties included the control and clearance of weeds and plants from the track. Standards of track maintenance improved steadily through the twentieth century, thanks to increased mechanisation, including the use of weed-killing trains, equipped with sprays designed to cover large areas of track. This 1920s Southern Railway promotional photograph shows a weed-killing train in action, in this case with old locomotive tenders converted into spraying vehicles. The foreman or manager, rather overdressed for the task, keeps an eye on things.

Replacing a Bridge, 1920s

Bridge replacement was a regular engineering challenge for railway companies. In the early days cast iron was used but this was quickly found to be prone to cracking and so wrought iron became the standard material for metal bridges until the coming of structural steel from the 1860s. A number of factors could bring about the need for a bridge to be replaced, including wear and tear, the laying of additional tracks or changes to the road or river being bridged. Then, as now, engineering work that involved track closure was generally carried out at night or over weekends, to reduce the level of disruption, and a well-planned bridge replacement could be completed in a day or so, thanks to prefabrication and the availability of modern engineering machinery.

This photograph shows such a process under way in the 1920s. The tracks have been lifted, but the new rails are ready for re-laying. The old bridge sections are being removed, while gangs of men prepare the ground to receive the new bridge, which is ready on the right, having been assembled from prefabricated sections brought to the site by train. When the time comes, it will be moved sideways into position, using cranes and hydraulic jacks.

The most extraordinary thing, bearing in mind modern health and safety regulations, is the way it has been turned into a major spectator event. Crowds of well-dressed spectators are standing around and watching, up close to the action. There is a group of schoolboys on one side, and other watchers are casually sitting on piles of timber. Some actually seem to be standing on the new bridge. Two policemen stand and chat, unconcerned about what is happening.

A Lofty Job at King's Cross, 1920s

London's King's Cross Station has long been regarded as a landmark in functional architecture, and hence is often seen as a precursor of the Modern Movement. In fact, its stark design by Lewis Cubitt for the Great Northern Railway was driven more by the need for speed and economy than any kind of architectural revolution. The plain brick façade fronted two great train sheds, each 800 feet long and 107 feet wide, covered by semicircular roofs built originally from timber, but soon replaced by iron. The only decorative detail was the Italianate-style clock tower, rising 120 feet above the station.

For a major station a well-planned maintenance schedule was essential. Much of this naturally concentrated on the areas used by trains and passengers, but equally important were the places outside the public eye, for example the roofs and the drains.

Most stations had clocks, and these had to run to time. After all, it was the timetable that determined the successful operation of the railway, and that was itself the greatest legacy of the railway age, the establishment of fixed time throughout Britain. Until trains ran regularly between, for example, London and Bristol, it did not matter that Bristol time was ten minutes different from London time. Therefore, clock maintenance was also an essential part of station life, as few passengers had access to clocks or watches. So, the several faces of the King's Cross clock were regularly cleaned, a necessity in the smoky atmosphere of Victorian London. This dramatic photograph, taken in the 1920s, is captioned, 'A lofty job at King's Cross. Cleaning the famous station clock.' At least the workman, perched precariously high above the station, is wearing a safety rope.

GOODS

Down Freight, Dainton Bank, June 1960

Most railways were built for the carriage of freight, or goods, with passengers a secondary concern, and until the 1950s, freight revenues were all-important. The transport of freight by train was the both lifeblood of industry and the national economy, and the key to the success of the village shop. Everything travelled by train, and so the smallest country station had a goods yard, or goods shed, and certainly a siding or two where wagons could be loaded and unloaded. The extensive, and usually efficient, railway bureaucracy enabled the movement of wagons and their contents to be documented and tracked across the country, from factory or warehouse to marshalling yard and thence to their destination.

Freight ranged from bulk loads such as coal, stone, oil products, milk, fish, mail and newspapers, which travelled in dedicated trains, to individual wagons carrying soap, foodstuffs, bicycle parts, clothing, writing paper and the myriad things that kept ordinary life operating smoothly. These individual wagons, the core of the freight traffic, travelled together in long trains known as mixed freights, a common sight throughout the railway network until the 1970s.

This photograph, taken on a bright summer's day in June 1960, shows the classic mixed freight, composed of a parcels van, a couple of containers, some box wagons, a plank wagon and a long rake of coal trucks, with the obligatory brake van at the end. Dainton Bank, south of Newton Abbot in Devon, is a famously steep climb for two miles, and always a challenge for a locomotive's footplate crew. Here, a Class 6800 locomotive No. 6875, *Hindford Grange*, from a group of eighty built by the GWR in Swindon between 1936 and 1939, hauls its train slowly up the hill, aided by a banker, a large tank locomotive at the rear.

Barnsley Interchange Junction, 1967

Like many places in Britain, Barnsley had two stations, built in the 1850s by competing railway companies. After various changes in ownership and name, they ended up in the 1920s as Barnsley Court House, operated by the LNER, and Barnsley Exchange, under the control of the LMS. Court House was closed in 1960, and Exchange was renamed Barnsley, but then, after a complete rebuild, became Barnsley Interchange. The Exchange name lived on informally, and was still in popular use in 1967, when this photograph was taken.

Main line steam ended in Britain in 1968, the conclusion of a process launched by the 1955 Modernisation Plan. By 1967 steam had disappeared from many parts of Britain, but it lingered on in some areas, mainly in the north of England. This richly detailed photograph captures the atmosphere of that time of change. Freight is still alive and sidings in the distance are filled with wagons of one kind or another. Below them, a dirty and unloved Black Five, No. 44857, a member of a large and famous class designed for the LMS by William Stanier in the 1930s, is shunting a single wagon. This locomotive, minimally maintained like others at that time, was withdrawn later that year, in October 1967, and scrapped. In the foreground two brake vans, still essential vehicles for all freight trains at the time, but soon to face a gradual redundancy, sit behind an equally uncared-for Class 37 diesel. Nearby is a diesel shunter. Tracks and platforms are overgrown and there is a sense of the untidy abandonment that affected parts of the network in that era, perhaps exacerbated by the knowledge that the railways were generally unloved in a period when road transport was dominant.

Coal and Smoke, Sandhole, 1960s

From the early nineteenth century, the movement of coal was the primary railway activity, with many lines being built specifically to connect mining regions to docks and harbours. Through the Victorian era the production of coal increased hugely, to cater for the needs of a burgeoning industrial economy that was wholly driven by coal, and to satisfy the ever-increasing demands of a major export business.

In order to meet these demands, collieries were opened wherever seams were deemed adequate. Typical was Sandhole Colliery, also known as Bridgewater Colliery, opened in Mosley Common, Walkden, near Manchester, in 1865. Well known for the high quality of its coal, the colliery was steadily expanded through the late nineteenth and early twentieth centuries. However, geological problems greatly increased costs and Sandhole was closed in 1962, though its washery remained open to serve other nearby collieries until 1968. Rail-connected like most collieries, Sandhole had a network of sidings to allow for the constant movement of empty and loaded coal trucks.

This winter scene shows an industrial saddle tank locomotive, perhaps part of the National Coal Board fleet, struggling to move a long line of loaded coal wagons to a point where they can be made up into a longer train for onward movement on the main line. Smoke and steam fill the cold air, a reminder of the harsh reality of a coal-fired world. In the distance beyond the bare trees a line of cottages can be seen, in which life must have been dominated by coal dust, dirt, smoke and noise.

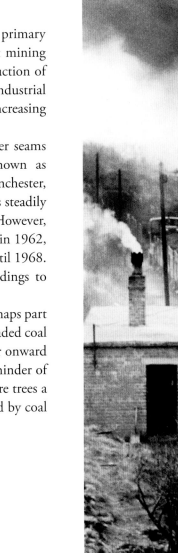

Pick-up Goods, Tongwynlais, 1950s

Until the 1950s many of the more remote parts of Britain were still rail-dependent for passenger travel and for freight. When the passenger traffic dwindled away, the movement of freight often continued. While the emphasis was inevitably on profitable main-line business British Railways still maintained an extraordinary network of local freight services, many of which lingered on until the late 1960s.

The backbone of these services was the pick-up goods, whereby a locomotive was despatched once or twice a week along a rural and remote line, collecting one wagon here, delivering another one there, and usually ending its journey at a large goods yard where wagons and their contents could be sorted and sent on their way to their ultimate destination. It was a slow and leisurely operation, often involving complex shunting operations at small stations or halts, or along a factory siding, with limited facilities and on poorly maintained track. The train crew – the driver, fireman and guard – were often the only railway employees present, and so they would have to look after the points levers, crossing gates and everything to do with shunting.

Tongwynlais station was on a secondary line north of Cardiff that had been opened in 1911. The primary aim was the transport of freight to Cardiff docks, but passengers were also carried until 1931, when the line closed. Having lain dormant for years, it was reopened again in 1947 for freight but had only limited use until it was closed again permanently. This photograph, taken shortly before the final closure, shows a pick-up goods struggling along the overgrown track towards Nantgarw. Today, Tongwynlais station is still standing, though long out of use. Little else survives, with much of the route under the A470.

An Exceptional Load, 1930s

In their heyday, railways could carry almost anything, from elephants for a travelling circus to complex castings and engineering products. Defined by law as 'common carriers', railway companies had in any case to accept whatever loads they were offered. As a result, there were ranges of special wagons developed for these tasks, the largest of which had fifty-six wheels and could carry 160 tons. Many exceptional loads were oversize, and so special routes had to be planned with sufficient bridge, tunnel and gauge clearances. They travelled mostly at night or during weekends, to minimise disruption.

A typical, and regular, client, initially for the North Eastern Railway and later for the LNER, was the Darlington Forge Company, established in 1854 and one of that town's heavy engineering pioneers. They specialised in the manufacture of complex cast and machined parts for large liners and warships, including rudder and stern posts, stems, crankshafts, guns and anchors, all of which were moved from their premises to the dockyards by train. Liners such as the *Olympic* and the *Titanic*, and battleships such as HMS *Prince of Wales* had components made by the Darlington Forge Company.

This photograph shows a typical exceptional load of ship components being transported by the LNER from Darlington to the dockyards on the Tyne. The weight, height and the width of the load would have been a challenge, resulting in careful route planning and train control, from the signalmen to the train crew. The date is probably the 1930s, though the extensive and impressive line-side planting of vegetables could suggest a later date, during the Second World War.

MADE BY
THE DARLINGTON
FORGE LD

Unloading Bicycles from a Container, 1930s

Today, much the world's railway freight traffic is container-based, using the range of standard shipping containers to transport all kind of goods over long distances and across international frontiers, on scheduled services.

However, there is nothing new about the container idea, and prints of railways such as the Liverpool and Manchester show specially made boxes being carried on flat wagons. Previously, similar things had been developed for canal boats. There were various other versions, mostly experimental, during the nineteenth century, but the idea really took off in the 1920s when competition from road transport forced the railways to be more efficient. Containerisation cut out the slow, laborious and expensive process of transhipment of freight between railway wagons. More important, railway containers were developed that could also be carried on lorries, making possible a door-to-door service. Particularly successful was the application of containers to the house and industrial removal business in the 1930s. These were iron-framed wooden containers of a standard size, designed to fit on both a flat railway wagon and a lorry, and equipped with chains to allow easy movement by crane. This traffic steadily increased, and in 1957 British Railways had 35,000 containers, many for particular cargoes such as foodstuffs and chemicals. Next came dedicated railway container services such as Condor, introduced in 1959, and Freightliner, from 1962.

This 1930s photograph shows bicycles being unloaded into a warehouse, perhaps in London, from a standard end-loading railway container, still sitting on the lorry that had carried it from the goods yard to its final destination.

Unloading Beer, St Pancras, 7 November 1958

Breweries and railways were mutually beneficial during the nineteenth century because the production of the former was hugely increased by the distribution of the latter. Over thirty breweries expanded from local into national names during the same period, largely owing to their railway connections, and many smaller breweries were built near railway lines. Brewers also began to buy public houses that were close to railway stations. By the end of the nineteenth century around 150 breweries had private sidings, though many were used primarily for bringing in coal and raw materials, rather than taking beer out.

Burton-on-Trent was the great centre of beer production, and the town was criss-crossed by sidings and private branch lines, much to the benefit of the Midland Railway. The fortunes of this company, formed from mergers in 1844, were based on the transport of coal, but beer also made a significant contribution, and so when the Midland was planning its great London terminus at St Pancras in the 1860s it made sure that these two commodities were adequately catered for. Adjacent to the station was a massive coal and freight depot, while the station's basement was turned into a huge beer cellar, into which loaded wagons could be shunted.

This 1958 publicity photograph shows this cavernous cellar, densely stacked with beer barrels and crates delivered directly from the breweries in Burton-on-Trent, a traffic still thriving in the era of British Railways. Today, this same space is filled with the shops, cafés, ticket desks and check-in terminals that serve international Eurostar trains, and the other railway companies now using St Pancras.

Mixed Freight, Peak Dale, Derbyshire, 22 September 1973

From the late 1950s freight traffic, and therefore freight revenues, began to decline all over Britain and this continued through the 1960s as the network was radically cut following the Beeching Report of 1963. Competition from road haulage increased year by year, and the railways were not helped by a government wholly wedded to the expansion of road transport, both private and commercial. Bit by bit the national network of goods yards, freight terminals, marshalling yards and dedicated sidings serving industry was demolished. Instead, the emphasis was on long-distance container trains and bulk cargoes such as coal. By the 1970s the traditional mixed freight train serving various local needs was facing extinction.

The Midland Railway, ever ambitious and competitive, had opened a new route from London to Manchester that passed through Derbyshire; one of its new stations, Peak Forest, opened in 1867. After a long life serving both passengers and freight, it closed in 1967, and its platforms were soon demolished. However, the Gothic-style station building survived and is still in use as an office for railway staff involved in modern bulk stone traffic from local quarries.

In this 1973 photograph a mixed freight of assorted open wagons is passing the remains of Peak Forest station, hauled by a Class 40 diesel locomotive, one of 200 built between 1958 and 1962. The many freight sidings around the station are still in use, though largely for storage. Notable are the number of brake vans, once part of every freight train, but by then being rendered obsolete by better braking systems and the rise of single-man operation of freight trains.

Coal for Export, 1930s

Railways were born to move coal, and this remained one of their primary functions well into the twentieth century. Railways and coal mining were mutually dependent industries and their patterns of growth were intricately interwoven. Railways not only moved coal from the pits to the docks, but also distributed it to every city, town and village on the network. Practically every station had a coal yard which served the needs of the local community. When the system was at its peak in 1913, the railways of Britain carried 225 million tons of coal. As late as the 1950s, the railways were still carrying 70 per cent of Britain's coal.

Much of the coal that was carried to the docks was exported, an international trade that grew rapidly during the nineteenth century. By 1900, 25 per cent of Britain's coal production was exported. In the 1930s, when this photograph was taken for the LNER, 15 per cent of coal produced from British pits was still being exported.

In this photograph, loaded coal wagons fill the sidings at one of the East Coast coal ports, possibly Sunderland, while ships wait at the quays. This was a familiar scene in many parts of Britain, and particularly where the coalfields were near to the sea, such as the North East, South Wales and parts of Scotland. The wagons carry the names of many collieries, for the mines were still privately owned, along with their fleets of coal wagons. Denaby is one name among many. This colliery was one of group between Mexborough and Conisbrough in the Yorkshire coalfield. Started in the 1860s, the colliery was famous for its deep shafts and its tempestuous industrial relations. A village, Denaby Main, grew up to serve the colliery. In the 1930s the pit was still in full production, with much of its output going for export. It closed in 1968.

HIGH DAYS AND HOLIDAYS
Your 1950 Holiday, Manchester Victoria

Railways and holidays developed together through the Victorian era. During the 1840s railways reached established resorts such as Brighton, Weston-super-Mare, Scarborough and Southport, and the day trip to the seaside was born. Next came the development by the railways of new resorts, for example Barry, Hunstanton and Saltburn. By 1914 the railway had reached around 200 places on Britain's coastline that could be regarded as holiday destinations. There were also many inland resorts, spas, historic towns, places for golf, walking and cycling, and mountain and moorland landscape. Railways made popular areas such as the Lake District and the remoter regions of Wales and Scotland.

The railways worked hard to promote the holiday potential of their routes. From the mid nineteenth century, some companies began to publish guidebooks and maps to tempt the holidaymaker, though this did not become a major business until the early years of the twentieth century. The GWR was a pioneer in this field, but others quickly followed. Annual holiday guides appeared and continued into the 1960s.

From the last decade of the nineteenth century, the railway poster became the most powerful promotional vehicle, thanks to greatly improved printing processes. By the 1920s a continual sequence of decorative, colourful and seductive images, many based on paintings by leading contemporary artists, was greatly improving the railway landscape. Stations became virtual art galleries, and remained so at least until the 1970s.

This 1950 display at Manchester Victoria was typical of those to be found at major stations. Among the destinations being promoted are Southport, Wales, Devon, Penzance, Torquay, Guernsey and the Isle of Man.

Carriage Sidings, Southport, 1950s

The railways had to manage the holiday traffic they had created. In the high season large numbers of special trains would bring thousands of holidaymakers and day trippers into resorts each morning, and then take them home again in the evening. At weekends the traffic could be even heavier. Station platforms had to be long and numerous, and the steady stream of arriving and departing trains controlled by complex signalling arrangements. Even more important were the acres of sidings required to store the holiday and excursion trains during the day. In some places dedicated stations were built to handle the holiday traffic. Much of this traffic was seasonal and so the special facilities had to be financed, built and maintained for the short period of use each year.

Southport had several stations, built by rival companies keen to benefit from the holiday traffic. The first railway arrived in 1848, initially with a terminus at Eastbank Street, replaced by Chapel Street in 1851. Next, in 1882, was the West Lancashire Railway's station at Derby Road, which later became Southport Central. Finally, grandiose Lord Street was opened in 1884 by the Southport & Cheshire Lines Extension Railway, designed primarily to cater for traffic from Liverpool. In 1901, following rationalisation by the now dominant Lancashire and Yorkshire Railway, Central was closed, with traffic concentrated at Chapel Street and Lord Street. In 1952 British Railways closed Lord Street, and from that point onwards Southport had one station.

This photograph shows the extensive carriage sidings at Southport Chapel Street, probably in the late 1950s, densely packed with the trains from the day's holiday and excursion traffic. An elderly tank locomotive is busy shunting. By the evening most of the sidings will be empty, ready for the next day's influx.

Dawlish, Devon, 17 August 1981

In 1846 the South Devon Railway's route from Exeter to Plymouth reached Newton Abbot. Isambard Kingdom Brunel tried out his atmospheric railway on this route, whereby trains were drawn along the track by a vacuum caused by differential air pressure in a tube laid between the tracks. Sadly, it was not a success and conventional locomotive haulage took over a couple of years later. The GWR acquired the South Devon Railway in 1876.

After leaving Exeter, the route follows the widening estuary of the river Exe, and then runs along beside the sea to Teignmouth. With the track nearly on the beach or winding its way through the cliffs, this is one of the most spectacular railway journeys in England. It has given pleasure to generations of holidaymakers bound for West Country resorts, many of whom must have been enjoying their lunch in the restaurant car as the sunlit sea views rolled past.

The sight of express trains racing along this seaside line has always attracted photographers, and tens of thousands of pictures must have been taken, dating back to the 1890s. Perennially popular were shots of classic, green-painted GWR locomotives bearing the names of kings, castles, halls and manors.

This photograph, taken on a lovely August day in 1981, shows Dawlish at its best. The station is in the distance and the beach is crowded with families and couples making the most of the sea and the sand. Others, clearly in holiday mode, stroll along the footpath that flanks the embankment. One railway enthusiast is seated on the wall, photographing the passing London-bound HST 125, widely promoted at the time by British Rail as 'the fastest diesel train in the world'.

Up the Posh, Football Special, January 1957

Railways and modern sports were both the creation of the Victorians and so there were inevitably close connections between the two. The rules of many popular sports were formalised during the latter part of the nineteenth century, notably rugby, football, athletics and tennis, but more important was the development of these and other sports as major spectator events.

Football and railways were particularly closely linked, for trains made possible the operation of leagues and national fixtures, with players and passengers being carried to and fro between matches. As early as the 1880s, at least 10,000 spectators were regularly attending games featuring major clubs such as Tottenham Hotspur, Aston Villa or Manchester United, all of whom travelled by train. Over 100,000 attended the 1901 FA Cup Final between Tottenham and Sheffield United. The successful movement of large numbers of people within a short period of time was one of the great achievements of the Victorian railways.

The same era saw the emergence of football specials, excursion trains dedicated to carrying thousands of football fans over long distances for low fares that often included the price of admission to the ground. For the next century these trains were an important part of the British football league programme, until widespread car ownership and, in their last decade, the rise of vandalism, brought the football special to an end in the 1990s.

This photograph shows a British Railways Class 4 locomotive hauling northwards a long train filled with Peterborough United supporters, on their way to watch their team play Huddersfield in the FA Cup on 26 January 1957. Sadly for them, the result was Huddersfield 3, Peterborough 1.

The Isle of Wight Ferry, 17 June 1960

The first railway-operated shipping route was launched in 1846 on the Humber. Others quickly followed, offering a variety of cross Channel, river, lake and even canal services for both passengers and freight. Between 1846 and 1984, when all remaining railway shipping services were sold off during the privatisation process, over sixty railway companies had operated well over 1,200 vessels of many different types. Apart from passenger and freight shipping services, railways also owned many other vessels, including canal barges, tugs and dredgers. Railways also pioneered the carriage of road vehicles on cross Channel routes, and British Railways introduced drive-on and drive-off ships in the 1950s. In 1970 all vessels operated by British Rail, from the largest cross Channel ferry to the smallest lake steamer, were given the new Sealink brand.

The Isle of Wight, where a railway network serving most of the island had gradually built up from the 1860s, was largely dependent upon railway-operated ships. The first scheduled service had started in 1817 but the railways were in control from the 1880s. Famous were the fleets of passenger-carrying paddle steamers, in service into the 1970s, along with the more basic but functional vehicle ferries and the pioneering passenger hovercraft.

This photograph, taken at Lymington, shows a Morris and a Ford being driven onto the nearly new MV *Freshwater*, a typical Isle of Wight vehicle ferry. A woman in a splendid period dress watches the proceedings. Built on the Clyde by Ailsa Shipbuilding in 1959, the *Freshwater* remained part of British Rail's ferry fleet until 1984, serving on the Lymington to Yarmouth route. She then returned to Scotland and was finally scrapped in 1997.

Camping Coach, Pateley Bridge, July 1934

In the early 1930s the Big Four railway companies began to think hard about ways of attracting holiday traffic. New hotels were opened, more excursions were advertised and the LNER launched the first cruise train, the Northern Belle. Less grand, but destined to be far more popular, were camping coaches.

The LNER launched the idea in July 1933, when ten old coaches were rebuilt for family camping, and placed on various scenic locations across the north of England. Well equipped and self-contained, though sometimes with limited water and sanitation, these were immediately popular as they offered an adventurous and cheap family holiday, at a cost of £2 10s a week. The LMS and the GWR introduced their versions of camping coaches in 1934, and the SR joined in a year later. By 1935 some 215 coaches were available at 162 locations all over Britain. Four years later, the number had risen to 439. The success of the scheme was based on the camping coach's broad appeal to families, camping enthusiasts, country lovers and people seeking a holiday with a difference. This continued until the early 1960s. The decline was then rapid, and British Rail closed their last camping coaches in 1971.

Railway companies made strenuous efforts to publicise their camping coaches. There were camping holiday guides and posters. Also popular were postcards, and the LNER issued this image in a series of promotional postcards from 1933. The caption stated: 'LNER Camping Coaches accommodate six persons and are equipped with every requisite for a camping holiday.' As there are at least eight people visible in the card, that coach must have been rather crowded. This was sent by some campers from their Pateley Bridge coach on 18 July 1934.

Open Day at Eastleigh, 9 August 1961

Throughout the nineteenth century the major railway companies in Britain generally built their own locomotives and rolling stock, and there were over twenty-five large railway-owned manufacturing works where quantities of steam locomotives were constructed. Many of these survived, in one form or another, into the British Railways era, with Swindon, Crewe, Derby, Doncaster, Stratford and Darlington becoming household names.

The appeal of railways, and steam trains in particular, seems to have been almost universal since the earliest days. Inevitably, railway works were particularly attractive places for enthusiasts, filled as they were with locomotives in various stages of construction and repair, and it was in response to this that railway companies arranged regular works open days. These occasions often attracted huge crowds, who mostly travelled to the works in special excursion trains.

In 1909 the London & South Western Railway moved its locomotive works to Eastleigh, near Southampton, where a new carriage and wagon works had been set up in the 1890s. Steam locomotives were made at Eastleigh until 1950 and diesels for a while longer. It remained a major repair facility into the twenty-first century. Eastleigh had regular Open Days, which always attracted large numbers of enthusiasts of all ages. Taken at an Open Day on 9 August 1961, this shows a well-turned-out 2-6-4 mixed traffic tank locomotive, No. 80152, from a British Railways Standard Class introduced in 1951. It is almost buried beneath a swarm of young enthusiasts. In the background other boys stand on the roof of a Class 08 diesel shunter, scenes inconceivable in an age now dominated by health and safety concerns. They are having a great time, with no railway official to be seen.

THE END

Sir Winston Churchill's Funeral Train, 30 January 1965

In 1854 the London Necropolis Company began to run scheduled services of funeral trains between their station at Waterloo and their cemetery at Brookwood in Surrey. This continued in one form or another until 1941, with coffins and mourners transported in special trains. Similar services operated elsewhere in Britain and in other countries, including Australia and Germany.

More important was the role played by the railway in state funerals. When Queen Victoria died her body was carried by train on 2 February 1901 from Portsmouth to Waterloo, and then on from Paddington to Windsor for her lying in state and funeral. Since then, the bodies of every British monarch have been carried to their funerals on special trains.

State funerals have also been awarded to politicians and other figures of note since the eighteenth century, with famous examples including Lord Nelson, the Duke of Wellington, William Gladstone and Earl Haig. The death of Sir Winston Churchill on 24 January 1965 set in train one of the largest and most impressive state funerals in history and the railway was at the heart of it. On 30 January a special train composed of Pullman carriages and a parcels van to carry the coffin set off from Waterloo, headed by Battle of Britain Class locomotive No. 34051, *Winston Churchill*, for the journey to Hanborough Station in Oxfordshire, the nearest to Bladon where he was to be buried. This photograph shows the funeral train passing Tilehurst, near Reading, with the coffin van behind the first carriage.

The End of the Line: Bankfoot Station, 20 April 1965

The Light Railways Act of 1896, which simplified the legal and constructional aspects of railway building and operating, was designed to encourage railways in rural regions by greatly reducing the costs. It was immediately successful, and over thirty railways were built under its regulations in many parts of Britain.

An early example was the Bankfoot Light Railway near Perth in Scotland, authorised in 1898, and finally opened in 1906. This short branch, which left the Perth to Forfar main line at Strathord Junction, was typical of many railways built under the Act. It existed to serve the local rural economy, and linked the small town of Bankfoot to the national network. The Caledonian Railway took control in 1913, and ran it until 1931, when passenger services ended. Freight survived a while longer.

Despite this early closure, Bankfoot Station and its engine shed survived for a long time remarkably unchanged, as this 1965 photograph indicates. Station, platform and engine shed are all intact, and there are even the remains of station notices and advertisements. Sleeper indentations still mark the track layout. Much of this continued to survive until the 1980s, surrounded by a caravan park, but the site is now covered by a housing estate.

Following the closure programme launched by the Beeching Report in 1963, scenes like this were soon to be found all over Britain, as the network lost 10,000 miles of railway and over 2,000 stations.

The Scrapyard, early 1990s

Though locomotives and rolling stock have often enjoyed long lives in service, most have eventually ended their lives in the scrapyard. Over the decades a few have always escaped, mainly ones considered to have some historical importance put aside for preservation. Survivors from the Victorian era are quite limited, but the twentieth century is well represented, thanks mainly to the rapid growth of preserved and heritage railways following the closure programmes of the 1960s and 1970s. While steam locomotives have generally been the preservers' main focus, rolling stock has also been important for the continued operation of historic and period trains on heritage lines.

During the 1960s, withdrawn locomotives and rolling stock were sometimes stored in railway yards and sheds before being taken to scrapyards in many parts of Britain. It was a thriving business, thanks to the massive scale of withdrawals during this period, but fluctuations in the scrap metal markets meant that most were quickly cut up. An exception was the famous scrapyard in Barry, South Wales, the final resting place for hundreds of steam locomotives, which were simply abandoned on the sidings for decades.

This photograph was taken at a scrapyard somewhere in Britain. Ready for the torch are piles of Mark 1 carriages, the standard type developed by British Railways in the early 1950s. Survivors are now the mainstay of the preserved railways and are regularly used on mainline steam and diesel-hauled heritage excursions. Two in the middle of the pile carry the Regional Railways livery introduced in 1988, a useful guide to the dating of the photograph. Among all the chaos, the remains of early diesel locomotives can also be seen.

Accident at Slough, June 1900

Accidents and disasters have always been a part of the railway experience. In the early days, these were very common, due largely to mechanical failure, inadequate signalling and train control, and, as ever, human error. Train travel in early Victorian Britain was, as a result, quite dangerous. A famous victim was Charles Dickens, who survived the boat train accident in Staplehurst, Kent, in June 1865, but never really recovered from the experience. Things improved steadily through the century, mainly because of increasingly efficient signalling, but disasters still occurred, along with a mass of minor accidents and incidents.

Britain's worst rail disaster was the multiple crash at Quintinshill, near Gretna in Scotland, on 22 May 1915 in which 226 people died, most of whom were Royal Scots soldiers on their way to serve in France.

This photograph shows the immediate aftermath of an accident on the Great Western main line at Slough. On 16 June 1900 an early afternoon express from Paddington bound for Falmouth ran through two sets of signals at danger before crashing into the rear of a local train that was stationary at the platform. Five people were killed and thirty-five injured. The locomotive from the express is buried in the pile of wreckage in the centre of the photograph.

The most astonishing thing is the group of passengers casually watching from the facing platform, several of whom seem dressed for a day on the river or at the races. Judging by the state of the wreckage, the accident can only have happened only hours before. Today, an accident is treated as a crime scene and guarded accordingly, and this kind of casual curiosity, though common at the time, is thankfully no longer possible.

PICTURE CREDITS

All images are from the author's collection. Several images within the collection can be additionally credited, as follows:

Page 1 Dundee freight: W. J. Verden Anderson; page 7 The Euston Arch: London Midland Region, British Railways; page 11 Bristol Temple Meads Station: P. J. Fowler; page 13 Peterborough North Station: Gerald T. Robinson; page 19 Tay Bridge: Valentine & Co., Dundee; page 20 Signal Gantry: D.H. Ballantyne; page 22 Tramway Junction: B. J. Ashworth; page 35 Fred and Jim at Crewe: J. R. Carter; page 41 Diesel Locomotive Driver: Western Region, British Railways; page 51 Eastbound Express: G. A. Richardson; page 52 Afternoon School Train: W. J. Verden Anderson; page 55 *Silver Jubilee*: British Railways; page 59 Stoke-on-Trent Locomotive Shed: R. Rushton; page 67 Weed-killing: A. E. Staples; page 78 Pick-up Goods, Tongwynlais: I. L. Wright; page 85 Unloading Beer: London Midland Region British Railways; page 86 Mixed Freight: C. Plant; page 89 Coal for Export: Turner & Drinkwater; page 91 Your 1950 Holiday: Kemsley Studios; page 93 Carriage Sidings: E. C. Morten; page 94 Dawlish: Melvyn Bryan; page 97 Up the Posh: Kenneth Field; page 98 Isle of Wight Ferry: Southern Region British Railways; page 101 Camping Coach: Joan Gurney Collection; page 105 Sir Winston Churchill's Funeral Train: Gerald Robinson; page 107 The End of the Line: Bankfoot Station: E. Wilmshurst; page 109 The Scrapyard: Gordon V. Allis.